How to live with yourself

DR. MURRAY BANKS

•

MURMIL ASSOCIATES, INC.
8 East 63rd Street, New York, N. Y. 10021

Copyright 1959, 1965

by

Dr. Murray Banks

All rights reserved.

The text of this publication or any part thereof may not be reproduced in any manner whatsoever without permission in writing from the author.

MURMIL ASSOCIATES, INC., 8 East 63rd Street, New York, N. Y. 10021

COMMENTS ON DR. BANKS' SAGE ADVICE... SUGAR COATED

By Dr. Morris Weintrob

Truth, often as bitter as some medicine, is frequently as helpful.

Physicians of today realize that it is unnecessary to prescribe the foul-smelling, foul-tasting concoctions of yesteryear solely for psychological effect.

In this age of "miracle" or "wonder" drugs, people take medicine no more willingly than did their forbears; but, young and old alike more readily swallow pleasant elixirs and insist that potions dispensed be sweetly flavored.

Dr. Murray Banks, whose vibrant growth into well-adjusted manhood the undersigned has watched with keen interest, has met increasing success as a popular lecturer on psychology. This has been well deserved.

He quickly gains the confidence of audiences, composed of varying gradations of intellectual receptiveness, *on the wings of laughter*, filling their minds and hearts with psychological truths by tactful approach and skilful delivery.

Often, his down-to-earth talks encompass so much of life's experiences within one short period that his enthralled listeners cannot believe that an hour has passed. One looks for the mythical seven league boots that enable him to traverse such far-flung fields in such seemingly limited time.

Like the astute doctor of medicine, Murray Banks *never talks down to his audience*, thus satisfying their collective ego. Furthermore, his observation . . . "we are all destined to be thwarted and frustrated in some things" . . . aptly captures the background upon which the modern psychosomatic concept of much of human sickness is based.

Emotional maladjustments producing a fractured sense of self-importance or a feeling of insecurity—frustration's common aftermath—frequently are evidenced by such non-organic physical disturbances diagnosed by thoughtful doctors of medicine as *nervous stomach, spastic or irritable colon, migraine headache,* and the like.

The surgeon is too often confronted with the diagnostic problem of differentiating between true physical disorders requiring use of the scalpel and bodily manifestations of emotional conflict.

Publications such as *How To Live With Yourself* do much to make life easier for physicians and surgeons. Dr. Banks, in his most effective style, dispenses bitter psychological truths coated with the sweetness of humor that makes them more readily acceptable. His readers cannot fail to respond satisfactorily to such skilful ministration.

Morris Weintrob, M.D., F.I.C.S.
Brooklyn, New York

A good reputation; a clear conscience; appreciation of nature; a peaceful heart; the knowledge of having given happiness to others; a trained and well-filled mind; satisfaction from duty well done; faith in the outcome of right; contentment; well-adjusted social relationships; these make for true happiness.

A Foreword By

DR. CLARENCE H. BELLINGER

Senior Director, Brooklyn State Hospital

The struggle of mankind for happiness has been a constant and engrossing one for centuries, probably since the advent of man on this earthly planet. Yet as we look about in this year of advanced civilization, we see unhappiness all around. In fact, there are those who say that as civilization continues, the woes and unhappiness of man increase. It is stated that man's accumulation of knowledge about his environment, the material and living things around him, has advanced far more than has his knowledge of himself. This is true but only in part.

Physicians have made many startling advances in the very recent past. Infectious diseases, which once ravaged the world, can now be brought under control, prevented and cured. Death from cancer or degenerative diseases can be prevented or at least delayed. As witness to this is the tremendously increased span of life to which the average person may look forward today. These advances have concerned primarily the illnesses affecting both mind and body.

Physicians have also learned much in recent years about the problems of human behavior, emotional reactions, habits of life, or the mind. They have attempted to publicize this knowledge with the result that at first it was met with resistance from some people. However, in more recent years this resistance has decreased with the result that much benefit has been derived from it. A greater interest seems to have developed among the people who wish to use this knowledge for their own benefit to reduce their woes and unhappiness. This process requires the application of an old saying, "Know Thyself." It means to understand why we behave (or react) as we do. Not just the first reason which comes to mind but the deeper and more nearly true reason. In this way behavior can be changed, not by law nor edict but by the individual himself. And he can live so as to increase his own happiness from within, the only true source of happiness. This is the purpose to which mental hygiene is dedicated.

CLARENCE H. BELLINGER, M.D.
Senior Director
Brooklyn State Hospital

I TAUGHT THEM ALL

I have taught in high school for ten years. During that time I have given assignments, among others, to a murderer, an evangelist, a pugilist, a thief, and an imbecile.

The murderer was a quiet little boy who sat on the front seat and regarded me with pale blue eyes; the evangelist, easily the most popular boy in the school, had the lead in the junior play; the pugilist lounged by the window and let loose at intervals a raucous laugh that startled even the geraniums; the thief was a gay-hearted Lothario with a song on his lips; and the imbecile, a soft-eyed little animal seeking the shadows.

The murderer awaits death in the state penitentiary; the evangelist has lain a year now in the village churchyard; the pugilist lost an eye in a brawl in Hong Kong; the thief, by standing on tiptoe, can see the windows of my room from the county jail; and the once gentle-eyed little moron beats his head against a padded wall in the state asylum.

All of these pupils once sat in my room, sat and looked at me gravely across worn brown desks. I must have been a great help to those pupils—I taught them the rhyming scheme of the Elizabethan sonnet and how to diagram a complex sentence.

NAOMI JOHN WHITE
Permission of the Clearing House

TO THE READER

There is a law in psychology that states in effect — "learning that is associated with pleasant feelings is the best kind of learning."

In my attempts to make learning as pleasant as possible, I have blended humor with psychology, only to find that people everywhere are hungry for knowledge of how to live better —but they want that knowledge presented dramatically and humorously. There are some things, after all, that are so sad that if we "did not laugh, we would surely cry."

"How To Live With Yourself" is a talk I have given numerous times with a great deal of gratification to many dozens of clubs and organizations. It is here published exactly as it was spoken.

Indeed, my greatest satisfaction has come when after my talk a member of the audience would say to me, "Thank you, you have made me laugh, and you have made me feel better."

That is what we all need — to learn each day how to live better and better — and to laugh as we learn it.

Eight East 63 Street
New York 21, New York

"Laughing is the sensation of feeling good all over but showing it particularly in one spot."

Laugh and Learn

*"To laugh is to be free from worry.
Who doesn't worry lives a long time.
To live a long time is to last.
Therefore he who laughs, lasts."*

HOW TO LIVE WITH YOURSELF

NO MATTER WHAT YOU DO IN LIFE, THERE IS A REASON FOR it. All behavior no matter how strange has its underlying reason.

At the funeral of the richest man in town a great many mourners turned out to pay their last respects to the dead. Among the multitude was a poor man who heaved deep sighs as he followed the hearse.

"Are you a close relation of the deceased?" someone asked him commiseratingly.

"I'm no relation at all!" he replied.

"Then why do you weep?"

"That's why!"

Although there is a reason for everything we do, the fascinating thing about human beings is that more often than not, we do not know the *real* reason for our actions. We think we know, and we are convinced of the motives for our behavior.

A woman goes to the gas company to pay her bill. She gets five dollars too much in change. But she'd like to keep it. So what does she say?

"They've got more money than I've got! They're all big crooks anyway. They must have gypped me many times. I'll keep it just to get even!"

Now is that the real reason she keeps the money? No. She simply keeps it because she wants more money.

The story is told of a man who has the habit of running around his apartment in the nude all the time, except for a high silk hat that he wears.

"Why do you always run around in the nude?" asked a friend.

"Oh, no one ever comes in here."

"Then why do you wear that high silk hat?"

"You never know," he replied, "when company may drop in!"

In my college classes I ask my students this question: "Tell me, how many of you expect to get married?" The hands go up. Selecting one boy, I ask, "Sam, *why* do you want to get married?"

Sam ponders and finally says, "Why? I never thought about it."

"Well, think about it, and tell me why you want to get married."

"Well," says Sam, "I want someone to love me; I want someone to cook for me; I want to have a place to come home to—in case I should decide to come home; I want—I want—I want."

To the girl: "Annie, why do you want to get married?"

"Well, I want to sleep late. I want to quit my job; oh, how I hate my boss! I want a man who will give me the things I've always wanted—furs, jewelry, nice things; I want—I want—I want."

So you see even when you get married, you do not marry for the reasons you give. Ask anyone why he got married. "Well, what else was there to do?" It is worth remembering, *No man ever marries just to be a good citizen!*

The real reason we get married is because we have certain wants, and we expect marriage to satisfy those wants. I have counseled many marriages—good and bad, and here is one secret of a happy marriage: KNOW WHAT YOU WANT OUT OF LIFE, AND SELECT A MATE WHO CAN HELP SATISFY SOME OF THOSE WANTS! Nothing could be more unfair than to attach yourself in a lifelong partnership *expecting* that certain wants of your personality will be satisfied, when from the very beginning it is impossible for the other person to do so.

If you are a very lively, enthusiastic, extravertive person, then don't marry someone who every three years—turns around! Imagine going to a show with such a person. What happens when you become enthusiastic, turn to him and say, "Isn't that wonderful! Joe, don't you think that's wonderful?"

Slowly he turns to you and says, "Everything to you is wonderful. Bah!"

What can you feel but, "Stay with me; I want to be alone!"

What Do Human Beings Want from Life?

Everything we do has a motive. Nothing is done without a reason. Whether we go to school, take a job, get married, stay single—everything has its motive. Now, what is it that all normal human beings want from life? What satisfactions are we striving for?

The whole drama of life springs out of four basic "I wants." Here they are:

1. I Want to Live

"How long?"
"Forever."
Oh, you will hear people say, "When I'm ninety I won't care if I'm dead!" And that is just the way you feel until you're eighty-nine! That's why people buy liver pills, patented cure-alls, washing machines. Did you think that a woman bought a washing machine to make clothes whiter? Oh, no. When the salesman says to the lady, "Madam, this machine will add twenty years to your life," she says, "I've got to have that machine, deliver it at once!"

2. I Want a Feeling of Importance

Everyone wants respect, power, prestige, admiration. Did you ever see a little boy who goes swimming or is about to dive?

"Watch me, Mama," he says. "Watch me!"

Now Mama can applaud and admire him. He glows under the admiration and approval. Adults are just the same. Of course we can't run around openly demanding, "Watch me, watch me!" Now we learn to do it more subtly. We do it with our big cars, expensive furniture, college degrees, furs, jewelry, diamonds.

A girl is engaged. "We're engaged, Annie," says Herman.

"We're engaged?" she answers. "Where's my engagement ring? Twenty-two carats, please."

This all calls: "Watch me, watch me—and admire!" There really is very little difference between infants and adults—although someone asked me once, "Do infants have as much fun in infancy as adults do in adultery?"

In connection with the feeling of importance—ego—what do you say when you are introduced to someone? Do you say, "How do you do?" If so, you will probably be forgotten in about five minutes, if it takes that long. What you should say if you can is:

"Oh, Mr. Appleduff—well—I've heard so many *nice* things about you!"

Then he spends half the night wondering what you heard, where you heard it, what's your name, and how can he find out what you heard! But don't say: "I've heard so many things about you." For if you do, he may think: "My God, maybe he knows!"

Be tactful. Tact is the oil of life. It makes the wheels go round smoothly and quietly. Oh, you can be rude, tactless, discourteous, and you will get on; but no one will like you. Tact makes the other person feel more adequate, and is related to the desire to feel important.

Of course it isn't so much *what* you say as *how* you say it.

A man died suddenly while doing business in the market place. So the minister sent the sexton to the dead man's wife.

"Be careful," he cautioned him, "and break the news to her as gently as possible!"

The sexton knocked. A woman came to the door.

"Does the widow Rachel live here?" he asked.

"I'm Rachel, and I live here," replied the woman, "but I'm no widow."

"Ha! Ha!" laughed the sexton, triumphantly. "How much do you want to bet you are?"

Perhaps another example of how to say it is illustrated in the story of the beautiful stage star who became greatly perturbed about her looks as she got on in years. Her photographer in particular began to feel the brunt of her temperamental moods. One day she was very unhappy over a set of photos taken of her, and she was furious with the photographer.

"What's happened to you?" she cried. "These pictures are awful. Where is that fine technique you had ten years ago?"

"Well, you must remember," the tactful photographer replied, "I am ten years older now."

A woman walked into a shoe store one day. She had rather large feet, but like many others with defects to which they are sensitive, she joked about it. To the salesman she said, laughing, "Can you fit a horse?"

The salesman looked her over carefully, and said, "Certainly, madam, sit right down!"

He might just as well have called her a horse! It is not what you say but how you say it. Why, take a little word like *No*. Did you ever consider how many different meanings "No" can have?

"No!" one man roars with fury in his voice.

"No, no," a mother cautions.

"Nooo—" a sweetheart coyly drawls. (This is probably the biggest *Yes* you'll ever hear!)

I remember overhearing a fellow trying to get a girl's phone number. "Come on, give me your number," he insisted.

"I will not," she insisted in return.

I called him over and said, "You know that's the worst technique I have ever seen."

"Why, do you have a better one?" he asked.

"Oh, yes," I told him. "You were *making* that girl say no. She couldn't say yes, because you were making her lose face. Whenever you embarrass another, make a person feel cheap or ridiculous, you will lose; you just can't win.

"But I will show you how you can always get yes for an answer, and here's how. Next time simply say, 'You know, I've enjoyed talking with you. I'd like to see you again sometime. Tell me, which is more convenient for you—shall I write or phone?'

"So she thinks, Which is more convenient for me—write or phone? Then she says, 'I think you'd better phone.'
"You come back with 'O.K., what's the number?'"
You must never give a person a choice between something and nothing. You might get nothing. Always give a person a choice between *something* and *something*—both of which are favorable to you.

If you say, "You wouldn't lend me five dollars, would you?" what can the answer be but, "That's right, I wouldn't. How'd you know?"

Say: "Which can you lend me, five or ten?"
"Here take five. This way you lose five and I lose five."
Let a person retain his feeling of adequacy and importance and you will always be better liked. For example when someone asks you an embarrassing question, don't offend his ego by saying "It's none of your business." Be like the Jew, who when the Irishman asked him, "Tell me, why do you Jews always answer a question with a question?", he replied, "Why shouldn't we?"

3. *I Want a Mate*

Everyone wants to be loved. Unfortunately there are more people who want to be loved than are willing to do the loving.

Said one girl: "I was involved in a triangle; he and I were both in love with him."

Every woman would like to marry well. Often a girl would rather remain single than marry *any* simpleton. She's waiting for a *special* simpleton! No wonder the poor woman in Baltimore who at the age of forty-four was called an old maid exclaimed:

"I am not an old maid. I'm an unclaimed treasure."

Perfume manufacturers know that women want romance. Did you ever notice the names on perfumes? "Desire," "Possession," "Tabu," "Risque," "Forbidden," "Unfinished Business"—"Follow Me," "Come and Get It"—"Evening in Paris." (Why not Evening in the Bronx? Don't they do the same things in the Bronx?)

Speaking of perfumes, I am told that there is a new perfume coming out called "Whiffenpoof"— One whiff—and poof! One fellow told me he expects to make a fortune on a new perfume.

Says it drives women crazy! Smells like money.

Everyone seeks for the security of a permanent and enduring love. One girl said to her boy friend:

"Tell me, Herman, do you love me?"

"Yes," said Herman.

"Would you die for me?"

"No, mine is an undying love!"

A durable and permanent love—this is a much sought after goal of so many humans. What is it we *want* in love, and what is it we *get* in love?

One fellow wrote to his sweetheart:

DEAREST ANNABELLE:

I would swim the mightiest ocean for one touch of your little hand. I would climb over mountains and valleys for one smile from your little lips. I would tramp over deserts for one twinkle from your little eyes.

Your everlasting slave,
OSWALD

P.S. I'll be over Saturday, if it doesn't rain.

I have mentioned three "I Wants"—I want to live and be healthy; I want a feeling of importance, power, prestige; I want a mate—love. What do you guess the fourth one to be? Money? No, not money. Money is only the means to satisfy the wants. It is because of what we really want that we seek money. Often we take what the money gets us instead of the money itself. Many a person has taken a job that paid less because it carried more prestige.

If you are thinking the fourth one is sex, then remember it comes under "I want a mate."

The fourth "I Want" is:

4. I Want a Little Variety—Change

Humans tire of the same things. We hate monotony, and seek through recreation and vacations to escape the sameness of our routine.

A woman goes to the closet packed with dresses, and murmurs, "I haven't a thing to wear."

Another says to her husband, "You know, Joe, I'm so tired of what I've been doing—always the same things. I'm tired of cooking the same dishes, making the same beds—to tell you the truth, Joe, I'm even a little tired of you. I think I'll go to the country for two weeks."

Speaking of variety, perhaps you saw Mae West in her show "Catherine Was Great." In one scene Mae saunters into her boudoir filled with at least one hundred men. She looks them over carefully, and drawls:

"I'm a little tired tonight. One of you boys will have to leave!" (Which may be carrying variety a bit too far.)

Frustration

All these things, human beings want—to live and be healthy; to be admired, have power, prestige; to find a mate and be loved; to escape from the monotony of life through variety. But—we are all destined to be thwarted and frustrated in some of these things.

The person you love, and who loves you, may die. The power you seek may never come. Ill health may threaten at every turn. Frustration is the destiny of man. Frustration will face you in some phase of life sooner or later, even though you be a multimillionaire.

I should like to protest now against loveless marriages. If you marry someone for money only, without love, well, the best I can say is, you will suffer—in comfort! But suffer you will.

One married woman said to me, "I'm suffering anyway, I may as well suffer in comfort."

In America a man has a very decided advantage over a woman in his love life. A man may be homely and getting on in years, yet if he wishes to get married he doesn't have very much trouble.

But a woman! A woman is a slave and a victim to her looks. Looks, looks, looks! The emphasis on a woman's looks has led to the choice of mates with qualities that do not necessarily make for a good wife or mother.

When a girl goes out with a homely fellow, what do people say? "He's got character! On him it doesn't show, but he's got it!"

But when a fellow goes out with a homely girl, what do people say?

"If Moses had seen her, there'd be another commandment!"

I remember a woman in her anxious thirties who sat in my office, and complained: "Dr. Banks, why do men find me so repulsive?" By the oddest coincidence, after she left, a man entered my office, and believe it or not, he said, "Dr. Banks, why do the women find me so repulsive?"

I thought, "Ah, I'll arrange an introduction."

I arranged the introduction, and what do you think happened? *They found each other repulsive!* It was very disheartening.

The difficulty of locating a proper mate has given rise to the interesting phenomenon of the "marriage broker." One marriage broker arranged a meeting with the following results:

"You faker, you swindler!" hissed the prospective bridegroom, taking the marriage broker aside. "Why did you ever get me into this? The girl's old, she's homely, she lisps, she squints."

"You don't have to whisper," interrupted the marriage broker, "she's deaf too!"

Adjustment to Frustration

We are all going to meet frustration in our lives. This we must realize at the outset. The important thing, however, is what you do when you are faced with failure, difficulty, scandal, or loss of a loved one through death. What you do—and every individual does something—we call by the term "adjustment." A situation demands an adjustment. And all of us learn to make varied adjustments to our daily problems. Some of the adjustments we make are good, some indifferent, and some useless, and even dangerous.

There has not been too much success in adjustment. Here are the most shocking figures you will probably ever hear:

There are 7,000 babies born in the United States every twenty-four hours. Of these 7,000 babies, one out of every 17 will be in a hospital for the mentally ill before his life is over.

There are more people in the institutions for the mentally ill than there are students in all our colleges and universities put together! There are more persons in beds for mentally ill than for all other hospital beds combined.

The American Medical Association reports that one out of every 13 men reporting for induction in the armed services was rejected as mentally unfit.

It has been estimated that out of a group of twenty-five children, 1 of the group will be in a hospital for the mentally ill before his or her life is finished; 4 more will be profoundly neurotic; 4 more will be deeply neurotic; 4 more will be mildly neurotic, and approximately 8 to 10 will be fairly normal.

Your chances don't look good, do they? That all depends on the kind of adjustments you learn to make. Adjustments are learned! We are not born knowing how to make intelligent adjustments.

Here is a case of adjustment: A case about a woman whom you probably know, and have heard about. This woman was in love—deeply in love, but was jilted by her sweetheart. She then committed suicide. Her name? Lupe Velez. Her name? Carole Landis. Remember?

Lupe Velez and Carole Landis had fame, fortune, beauty;

everything that many women would give half a life to have. But when they lost their sweethearts—Lupe left a note:
"Dear Harold:
There is nothing left for me anymore, so good bye to you."
I wish she had phoned me first. I'd have given her some good ideas.

Did you know that Lupe Velez and Carole Landis were insane when they killed themselves? Only the insane wish to die. I am not speaking of those who regularly commit suicide each week, who proclaim loudly that they would have been dead, except for the horrible odor of the gas. Real suicides are always mentally ill. Sane people wish to live.

A man was carrying a heavy load of wood on his shoulders. When he grew weary he let the bundle down and cried bitterly, "Oh, Death, come and take me!"

Immediately, the Angel of Death appeared and asked, "Why do you call me?"

Frightened, the man answered, "Please help me place the load back on my shoulders."

Even though life has its griefs, man prefers a life of wretchedness to death.

It is believed that anyone who goes insane over failure in love was insane to begin with. After all if everyone who were to fail in love were to go insane, who would be left to take the case histories of those who were going insane?

When her sweetheart left her, a Japanese girl wrote to her American soldier boy friend:

DEAR HARRY:
You are gone three months, and I am three months gone. What shall I do? Shall I commit Hari Cari, or shall I carry Harry?

Of course, not every girl who falls in love wants to kill herself. Some say, "Why should I kill myself? I'll shoot him!" Thus even murder is a form of adjustment. (She adjusts him pretty permanently, too.)

Some people when faced with trouble turn to liquor to wash away their troubles. Liquor will never wash away your troubles.

It will only irrigate them a little bit. One man said, "My father is a drunkard. He read a sign, 'Drink Canada Dry.' So he went up there to do it."

Once there was a scholar who was a souse. A friend rebuked him:

"Don't you know that our sages condemned drunkenness?"

"Do you need to tell me that?" retorted the scholar. "Of course, I know. I'm not drinking to get drunk, but to drown my sorrows!"

"Have you succeeded in drowning them?" the friend asked.

"No, I'm afraid not," the scholar answered grimly. "You see my sorrows are very spiteful. The more I drink the better swimmers they become!"

Some people turn to insanity as an *adjustment*. Insanity is a form of adjustment to an intolerable life problem, as I will illustrate later. Thus a person who goes insane may even be thought of as wanting to be insane. Now when I say *want to be*, I don't mean that this is a forthright decision which is consciously made. A man or woman doesn't sit down and say, "I think today I'll go insane." It is the eventual outcome of a series of ineffective and dangerous adjustments which the individual has learned to make as part of his pattern of life.

Forget the delusion that people are born insane. We do not inherit insanity. The most we can inherit is peculiar parents! Although, of course, then our chances are much better.

We *learn* our patterns of adjustment, and parents play an important role in this respect. It has been wisely said: "The best break a child gets in life is when he selects good parents." That's the first real break.

Of course you have heard the term "nervous breakdown." This is a very widely used expression. Perhaps your mother had one. Your father? Your sister? Your husband? Perhaps even you had one. A "nervous breakdown"! We all know what that is.

But did you know that *there is no such thing* as a "nervous breakdown?" The nerves, never, never, break down! Yet there are thousands of patients—thousands upon thousands—who visit doctor's offices and complain: "Doctor, I've got weak nerves—weak nerves! I need a nerve tonic. Something with iron in it."

He may as well give you Fitch's Shampoo for all the good it

is going to do you. What are weak are not your nerves, but your habits of adjustment!

What do human beings do with their fears? We take fear of death, fear of old age, fear of losing money, fear of being found out, fear of failure, FEAR, FEAR, FEAR—and we turn it into a "nervous stomach," "weak heart," "headaches," "constant tiredness." A person complains, "I don't know why it is, but I'm always tired. No matter how much I sleep, I'm tired." People are constantly turning their fears and conflicts into physical aches and pains. Daily, thousands of X-rays are taken for aches and pains that exist in the emotional life of the patient, not in the organs. Oh, the pain is real enough, and it hurts as strongly as if it were caused by a real infection—but its cause lies in the fear and conflict which the patient is battling.

How does a situation like this occur? Why do people convert their fears into bodily disturbances? To understand this, you would have to look into the home life of a child to see how he *learns* his particular adjustment to his daily problems.

Let us look into the home of little Joe, aged ten: He gets up one morning, eats a hearty breakfast, and on the way to school he suddenly remembers that he has an arithmetic test to take. He thinks: Maybe I should throw up? Then I wouldn't have to take the test! But he manages to keep it down. In the classroom you can observe him doing the arithmetic problems, but then the third problem is too difficult—so phfft . . . That's all!

The principal sends him home. Mama puts him to bed. Papa buys him a toy. Sister reads him a story. Why, the upset stomach has had a high value! He has saved face.

If he had come home with a mark of 50 on his test, what would

Mama have said? "Why are you so stupid? Why can't you be smart like the little boy next door?"

In this case, however, she says, "Imagine how smart my little Joe must be. Even though he was sick he managed to get fifty. Can you imagine what he would have gotten if he weren't sick! He must be a genius. Isn't that true, Joe?"

"Yes, it's true. I am very bright. But I'm sick. That's why I got fifty."

Now, little Joe is big Joe, and whenever he meets a problem that is too much for him he throws up without even thinking about it. He goes from doctor to doctor complaining of "nervous stomach." But can't you see that his nervous stomach is a protection? A protection from the truth, which is: Joe, you're a flop! With his "nervous stomach" he says to the world: "World, look at me, World, I could be a such a success. I'm really quite brilliant, but my nervous stomach—that's what prevents me." And Joe would rather suffer from all the misery of the stomach disorder than face the real truth—that he is a failure!

More or less, all of us learn to turn our dissatisfactions and emotional tensions into physical complaints. It is a form of neurotic escape. Notice how tired *you* get whenever you have something unpleasant to do.

How do you feel when someone says to you, "Come inside, help me clean up the house?"

"Oh, I'd love to, but I'm so sleepy. I just can't keep my eyes open. I've got to lie down for two months."

But notice how wide-awake you feel when someone invites you to go to a night club or the theater!

Even in our speech we show the tendency to convert our emotional tensions into physical ones:

"I hate her. She just makes me burn up inside!" (Now you have taken a hate, and turned it into a heartburn!)

"I don't like him. He gives me a pain in the neck!" (Sometimes we locate the pain in other places!)

Examples of Neurotic Adjustments

Here is a case of a so-called "nervous breakdown." I remember interviewing a very attractive young girl of twenty-one who was deeply in love with a young, poor sailor, whom she wanted to marry. Her mother, however, had other plans. She wanted her daughter to marry a very rich, but rather old man. (Of course, Mother didn't want her to marry him for his money, but she didn't know how else to get it.)

She and her daughter argued constantly until Mother had a "heart attack" and finally won. The daughter agreed to break off her relationship with the sailor and marry the old man.

The wedding was held at the Waldorf-Astoria Hotel in New York City. It was a beautiful wedding, and the bride looked stunning.

But as she walked down the aisle to the altar—ten feet before she reached the altar she fell to the ground paralyzed from the hips down, and was carried off in a stretcher.

Of course, if you wish, you can call this a "nervous breakdown." But I assure you, not a single nerve broke down. Not one! And all the injections, pills, or physical treatments in the world will not cure this girl. This represents her unconscious, neurotic, hysterical adjustment to a miserable life problem. Now that she cannot walk she cannot reach the altar and complete the marriage. She is not faking a paralysis at all. She is genuinely paralyzed. But the paralysis itself is her own unconscious adjustment to this problem, and will never show up on an X-ray.

Here is another illustration: A skin specialist asked me to talk with a woman who had a chronic skin rash, which stubbornly resisted all treatment. He felt that there was an emotional reason that aggravated or caused her skin condition.

I did not get very far with her, but one day her husband left her, and when he left, the rash left too! This woman was allergic to her husband! She hated him, yet could not be divorced because of her religious feelings about divorce. At the same time, however, she was emotionally attached to another man whom she really wanted to marry. The rash was the outward expression of her internal conflict. Again, an emotional conflict turned to physical symptoms.

The "Retreat into Insanity"

There is still another adjustment which is even worse than the psychoneurotic adjustments outlined above. That is the adjustment of insanity or psychosis. Even insanity is a form of adjustment, which is less painful than facing intolerable realities of frustration and denial.

I am thinking now of a girl who stands in the wards of a mental hospital in Brooklyn. She stands with her head bowed low, her hands at her sides, her face expressionless and empty. This is the way she has been standing for over sixteen years! In all that time she has not said a single word, nor voluntarily eaten a single thing. She is fed through a tube or she would die. If you pick her up, she stands up. If you throw her down she lies down. If you jab her with a pin, she allows you to do it, without an utterance of pain. Yet this girl is aware of what you are saying, and what you are doing. She feels the pain, and hears your questions, but she refuses to say or do a thing. She is not unusual. She is only one of thousands of boys and girls who stand in a similar way in wards of mental hospitals all over the country—standing like human vegetables—average age twenty-one or twenty-two. Human beings who have found the battle of life too much, and have retreated from the unpleasant realities by running into insanity.

How does such a thing happen? What makes an individual turn to psychosis as an adjustment?

This girl's present condition is a form of adjustment. But adjustment to what? What sort of thoughts did she have that makes such a retreat so alluring?

If we could look into her mind, perhaps we would observe the following:

My sweetheart has left me. I can't keep a sweetheart. I'm not pretty. No one will ever love a homely girl like me. Why, even my mother doesn't love me as much as she loves my little sister. My sister is pretty. She has curly hair, and everyone is always praising her. But no one ever notices me, except to tell me how stupid I am. My father says that I'm very stupid; that I'll never be anything.

How will I ever get a job? Who would take a stupid, homely

girl like me? I am afraid to even ask for a job.

I'd love to get married, but who would marry me? I won't even go to a dance. What if someone should ask me to dance, and I should make a mistake. Then they'd all laugh at me. Everyone would say how stupid I am. I can't bear to have people laugh at me.

Oh, how I hate this world. I'm afraid of it. I wish I could leave it. I do want to leave. Yes, I will leave. I'll go where no one can call me stupid, or laugh at me. I'll go where I don't need any sweethearts; where no one can hurt me. I'll go where I don't have to be smart, attractive, or loved. I'll give it all up, and leave.

And now she retreats like a little turtle into her shell, where she removes herself from the competition of life. Now no lover, mother, father, or employer can hurt her again. She has withdrawn from reality, and is immune to laughter, criticism, or love. She has become a human vegetable!

And *all of this could be avoided,* if we would only learn the effective principles of mental hygiene in time! What is mental hygiene? It is simply the learning of effective patterns of adjustment, so that when frustration and difficulty face us we do not run into psychotic or neurotic retreats. Mental hygiene is an *attitude,* a way of looking at life.

Perhaps one of the best definitions of mental hygiene that I ever saw appears on a menu of a restaurant where they specialize in doughnuts. This is what is written:

> As you ramble on through life, brother,
> Whatever be your goal,
> Keep your eye upon the doughnut,
> And not upon the hole.

One girl loses a sweetheart and she kills herself. Another girl looks for another sweetheart! Mental and emotional habits of adjustment: one healthy, one disastrous. After all there is no one person in the world for anyone. Poets may write of the "one and only," but psychologists know that whomever you marry is merely an accident of geography. If you live in New York you will probably marry a New Yorker; in Boston, a Bostonian; in Michigan, a Michigander.

When his wife died, a man had engraved on her tombstone "My light has gone out." A year later he was about to remarry, so he went to the bishop and asked: "Bishop, don't you think I should erase the inscription? It doesn't fit my present condition."

"No, no," said the bishop, "just write underneath: 'I have struck another match.'"

The Well-Adjusted Personality

After one of my lectures a woman came up to me and said, "Dr. Banks, I want you to show me how I can become *permanently* well adjusted."

"My dear lady," I replied, "the only *permanently* well adjusted people I know of are in cemeteries! There you adjust them once, and they stay adjusted! But so long as you live you have new and constant adjustments to make."

People say, "How do you like that! I just finished solving one problem, and now I've got another. Why is it that problems are always happening to me?" Because you are still *alive*, that's why. Life and problems are synonymous.

It wouldn't be good to be too well adjusted anyway. If you were completely pleased with yourself, you would never care to do anything to improve. We need to learn to be happily maladjusted! A good example of this is the wonderful philosophy of one milk company which paints this slogan on every one of its milk bottles: "Our cows are *not* contented. They are anxious to do better!"

What Is Normal?

Haven't you ever thought that you were abnormal? Haven't you ever suspected that your mental processes were not as "normal" as you felt they should be? Of course you have. We all have.

But what is normal? Who is normal? How can you tell what is normal? What is it that the insane do, that you do not? Actually nothing—but the only difference is they do *too much* of it, or at the wrong times. Normalcy is not so much what you do, but how much of it you do, and when.

To illustrate: Surely you have moments of depression—the blues. Of course you do, and that is normal. But you don't *stay* depressed. If you did, then the mental hospital would send for you. There are times too when you are highly elated and very enthusiastically happy. But if you stay too elated, or too happy, then the mental hospital sends for you too! Normalcy is not so much a question of *kind* of behavior as *quantity*.

You can be considered normal and healthy if you learn to meet all your problems in a realistic way, without retreat from reality, and without hurting others. Learn to secure your satisfactions from the real environment, rather than from too many dreams. Dream, but make your dreams come true, and "do not let your dreams become your master."

Speaking of who is sane and who isn't, the story is told of a man who was walking by a mental hospital with a sack on his back. A patient looking out of the window, saw him, knocked on the window and said,

"What you got there?"

"Fertilizer," answered the man.

"What's it for?"

"To put on my strawberries."

"Oh," said the patient, "I put cream on mine, but I'm crazy."

There are people who feel that others hate them, are trying to put them out of the way, are persecuting them, and interested only in destroying them. This condition is called paranoia. The mental hospitals are filled with such people.

One man of thirty-two said to me, "My mother is poisoning me."

"Really?" I asked. "How long has she been poisoning you?"

"Ten years."

"How come you're not dead yet?"

"It's a slow poison."

While there are paranoids in mental hospitals, all normal people are a little bit paranoic. Ask any son-in-law about his mother-in-law and you will note a little touch of paranoia. Or for that matter ask the mother-in-law.

A very good illustration of paranoid reaction is shown in the story of the lady who went to see the races. At the track, before the race began, she tapped a gentleman on the shoulder and asked:

"Could you please lend me a safety pin?"

"Sorry, miss, I don't have one."

Suddenly over the loud speaker the announcer cried, "THEY'RE OFF!" And she fainted!

Appraise Your Personality

At this point, I should like to ask you a very important question. If you want to know whether you are physically healthy, what do you do? You go to a doctor. He examines you. He takes your blood pressure, listens to your heart, and you find out if you are physically healthy. But what do you do if you want to find out whether you have a healthy personality? How do you find that out?

A woman may have a peaches-and-cream complexion, a gorgeous figure; a man may have muscles that bulge, together with the strength of Hercules; but—inside there may be a broken, twisted, miserable soul.

Here are some "indicators" to help you to appraise your own personality to see to what extent you make a good father, a good mother, a good husband, wife, or sweetheart.

I am going to ask you ten questions—ten little questions that will indicate how well adjusted you may be. The answers to these questions will show whether you know *how to live with yourself*. And you've got to know how to live with yourself before you'll ever be able to live with anyone else.

When a doctor of broken bodies comes to see a patient, he first inserts a thermometer. He wants to see how high the temperature is. A high temperature is the sign of a disease process in the body.

When a doctor of "broken personalities" examines a patient, he also has a thermometer, but it isn't made of glass. It's in the form of a question. Here is the question:

1. *Are You Happy?*

"Happy? I'm miserable, just miserable."

Such an answer indicates that you have a high "personality fever," and that you are not making the most effective adjustments to your everyday problems. Happiness is something that comes as a *by-product* to effective striving for desirable goals. It is never something that you can get directly. It is always a by-product of good adjustments and good living.

Don't confuse happiness and pleasure. Pleasure you can buy. You can buy an evening in a night club or a theater. You can buy a week in the country. But you can't buy happiness! When will human beings learn that? Happiness can't be bought. It must be lived!

If your life has purpose, if you set up desirable goals, and then work to attain these goals, then happiness comes to you—it comes to you as a by-product—your reward for good living.

2. *Are You Ambitious for Life?*

At any age from two to ninety-two are you interested in life, in love, in work, in play? Do you have zest for living? Are you interested in increasing your knowledge, in enriching your personality?

I have known people of 80 and 90 years of age who were very young. I have also known people of 18 and 19 years of age who

were very old. Now and then you will read in the newspapers of a boy of 19 who kills himself, by his own hand—finished, life spent, like an old, old man.

Said Oliver Wendell Holmes:

"To be 70 years young is sometimes far more cheerful than to be 40 years old."

There are people at all ages whose zest for living has long since disappeared, who eke out an existence, and can never be said to be living. Life is not something we find. Life is something we create! The truth of the matter is that it is existence that we find.

Be ambitious for life, but not ambitious beyond your ability. A parent should not attempt to fit a square peg in a round hole. Only tragedy can result when you try to make an engineer out of a moron.

Be ambitious within the limits of your ability, interests, and capacities. Always remember the little story I am about to tell you, should you desire to bite off more than you can chew.

A psychiatrist is speaking: "It was a year before the great depression that a gentleman came to me complaining of all the symptoms of nervous unrest and worry. He was in a dilemma.

"'I have a partner,' he told me, 'and we are doing a good business. My partner refuses to keep books. He just buys and sells and takes the profits. I told him a thousand times that we have got to keep books because we must pay taxes. He says if I don't like the way he does business, we should dissolve the partnership. So I talk it over with my wife and she said to me, "William, you can't do business with a man who doesn't keep books. It says in the Talmud: Don't push me too high; don't push me too low; let me go the even way."

"'Now, Doctor,' continued William, 'my partner is a very shrewd businessman and I hate to dissolve the partnership, but my wife, she can't respect a husband who isn't an upright citizen. As a result, I don't drink, I don't sleep. I don't know what to do.'

"My answer was quick: 'Break your partnership—your wife is right.'

"About a year after the depression, William came in to see me again. He walked with a slight limp. I asked him what was wrong with his gait and he told me the following story:

"'Doctor, I took your advice and dissolved the partnership. My partner made a million dollars, and I made a hundred thousand. I was satisfied. We moved into the same apartment house. His apartment was a penthouse with a terrace and my wife and I had an apartment on the first floor. My partner had two cars and a chauffeur—I had a nice little car which I drove myself. And again, I ate, I drank and I slept. "Don't push me too high, don't push me too low, let me go the even way" was good advice.

"'Then came the depression! My partner jumped out of the window and broke his neck. When I jumped, I only broke my ankle!'"

The moral to this story needs no further comment. Be ambitious but don't frustrate yourself by setting impossible goals.

On the other hand though, I remember a man who sat in my office one day, and on the way out sighed, "You know, Dr. Banks, I wish I had gone to college."

"Well, why don't you go?" I asked.

"Because I'm thirty-five years old, married, have two children, and it would take me ten years to go through college at night."

"Tell me," I asked, "how old will you be in ten years if you go?"

"Why, I'll be forty-five years old!" he exclaimed.

"And how old will you be in ten years if you don't go?"

He thought a moment and said slowly, "Uh, forty-five, I guess," and was completely confused that the age came out to the same amount.

Remember next time you say to yourself, "Oh, I can't do that, I'm too old," ask yourself: "How old will I be if I don't do it?"

And if you get a younger answer, please write or phone me immediately!

Did you ever want something so badly that you prayed for it, saying, "Please God, just send me this *one* thing, that's all I'll ever want!" And then you get your wish, and suddenly you go back to God and say, "Excuse me, God, I just remembered three more things!"

Next time you feel that there is only one thing that you will ever want, read this little poem to yourself. It has been a favorite of mine for many years. Perhaps you will see people that you know in it.

SEVEN DAYS

Before he was old enough
To know what God meant,
He began pestering Him.
On the First Day
He asked Him for something,
   praying:
"Dear God,
I'll never ask for anything
   again
As long as I live,
If only this once . . ."
He was a child then,
Wanting a bicycle for
   Christmas.

On the Second Day,
He prayed, saying:
"Dear God,
Never again will I ask . . .
But this time . . .
Please . . ."
He was a student
Asking for a passing grade
In higher Mathematics.

On the Third Day,
He prayed the prayer again,
But without realizing what
   he said,
Because he was thinking
Of Her.
"All I'll ever ask of you
Is Her."
He begged.
So God gave Her to him.

On the Fourth Day,
He became a father,
And God was once more
   requested
To guarantee the results.
". . . Though never again a
   favor,"
He promised.
But God was a little skeptical
   by now.

On the Fifth Day,
It was at a business
   conference,

When he felt another moment
   of inadequacy
And called upon God
To carry him through the
   crisis.
"Is this the last time?",
Asked God.
"Oh, yes," was the answer.
"Very well," said God,
And performed another
   miracle.

On the Sixth Day
He was an old man,
Very old and very senile,
But he still clung to Life,
And was afraid of Death.
And he began:
"Dear God,
I'll never ask for anything
   again
As long as I live . . ."
"That's true,"
Said God.
And he died.

And on the Seventh Day
God rested.

3. Are You Socially Adjusted?

Do you like people? Do you want praise, sympathy, understanding from others? Do you like to be in the company of other people? Do you get along well with others?

Social adjustment is imperative for good mental hygiene. In the last analysis the insane are those who can no longer get along with other people.

A person who hates people and who enjoys living a solitary life is a mentally sick individual.

You needn't be a social butterfly, but you should be adjusted to some congenial group.

4. Do You Have Unity and Balance?

Unity means that you are not torn between choices, that all your actions lead to the formation of a well-integrated personality and orderly thinking.

Perhaps the opposite of unity can be seen in the case of a woman who is on a reducing diet. Suddenly she is served strawberry shortcake. She eats it and thinks: Oh, am I gaining weight! I know I'm putting on pounds, and it worries me. (Waiter, another piece, please.) Oh, how I'm gaining weight! And so she eats it, and worries.

Now, if you are going to eat it and worry, then don't eat it! If you do eat it, then enjoy it.

Speaking of unity, one young man said to a girl: "So help me, I'll kiss you!" She replied, "So kiss me, I'll help you!"

Balance means that you are moderate in all things. That you are not irritatingly quick, or annoyingly slow. Balance means that you do not spend all your time in work or all your time in play. It means that you know when to play cards, and when to stop playing cards. It means that you know when to choose participating in a ball game, and when to attend a lecture.

Balance means that you do not wrap your entire life around one thing exclusively, like your mother, your father, your wife, your husband, your child, or your job.

If you do that, just consider what you are doing! You are setting your entire personality up on one single support. Would you build a house on one support and expect it to survive?

If you should ever lose that one support, then Heaven help you—you will collapse! You have nothing else. But if you have many interests, many activities—many supports—then if you lose one, or two, or even three, you won't go to pieces; you will be supported by your other interests.

Don't lose your balance by attempting to please everyone. If you feel that everyone must like you, must admire your talents or comment favorably on your clothes, then you will end up as a good neurotic.

Don't feel devastated when you hear that others are criticizing you. I think the first real sign of success is shown when others start criticizing and tearing you down. Criticism is usually a sign that you are alive and doing things.

Dr. A. A. Brill was once advised to go study with Freud.

"Who is Freud?" he asked.

"Oh, he must be someone of great genius; everyone talks against him."

5. Do You Give Attention in Your Life to the Present?

Oh, the thousands of people who make a hell on earth, worrying whether they will keep out of hell. We make a hell on earth by worrying over our past, over the things we did twenty years ago, by regretting and regressing, by wishing we could do it over, or undo it all.

"If I could only live my life over again, I wouldn't make the same mistakes twice." Of course not, you'd make a whole set of new ones!

We worry about the uncertain future. Will I make it? Will I lose my money? Will I ever succeed? Will I ever marry? Maybe my sister will marry before I do. Worry, worry, worry. Worry over the past, worry over the future—and no consideration for the present.

Consider: How many things that you worried about last year actually came true? There is a little saying that I have always been fond of: "I am an old man, and have had many troubles, most of which have never happened."

A group of relatives were gathered in the lawyer's office, waiting for him to open the envelope that contained their late relative's will.

The lawyer opened the envelope and read to the expectant group:

"Being of sound mind, I spent all my money while I was alive."

6. Do You Have Insight into Your Own Conduct?

This question is perhaps one of the most important of them all.

I once asked my students what the opposite of insight was. In chorus they called: "Outsight."

Insight is the quality of being able to see into yourself and see the truth. It means that you understand the deeper and real reasons for your behavior.

Did you ever wonder what a psychiatrist does with a patient? How he cures a patient? It is the psychiatrist's function *to help you to help yourself.* He doesn't attempt to cure you. He helps you to help yourself! But of course, if you do not wish to help yourself, then you are lost. A broken personality is not like a broken bone, where a splint can be placed, the finger bandaged, and it will get better in spite of you. In broken personality, you must want to be helped.

But if you do, then remember that all emotional problems, all nervous troubles of a psychological origin, are removed in two steps.

STEP 1. You are 50 per cent better when you get real insight—when you know the truth about your "nervous stomach," for example. When you realize that your stomach troubles you, not because you have a bad digestion, but because you are *afraid*—afraid of something, and for which the "nervous stomach" is a cover-up, a symptom. Then you are 50 per cent better. The proper diagnosis is half the cure. But if that is half the cure, what is the other half?

STEP 2. You are another 50 per cent better, when you give up the old ineffective adjustments (like a "nervous stomach") and turn to more realistic, more effective adjustments. Now you are 100 per cent better.

Yet there are people who say, "Oh, what I don't know won't hurt me. Ignorance is bliss."

Let me emphasize as strongly as I can that the only thing in this world that can ever hurt you is not what you know, but what you don't know! What you don't know can crush and destroy you. What you know, you can take care of. Ignorance isn't bliss! It's the most expensive and dangerous thing in the world!

The Bible gives you the answer: *Know ye the truth and the truth shall make you free!*

And this is the cornerstone of all psychiatry—for when the patient begins to know the truth, then he is on the road to recovery.

Yet, isn't it strange that there are "none so blind as those who will not see?" The mind is useless if the eyes be blind!

A professor was attempting to illustrate to his class the effects of alcohol on the human body. He placed a worm in a glass of water, and the worm crawled out. He then placed the worm in a glass of alcohol, and it was killed.

"What's the moral?" asked the professor.

A student called out, "I see if you drink alcohol, then you never have worms!"

There are none so blind as those who will not see!

Investment in knowledge always pays. Real estate may go down, stocks may crash, and the money you have so earnestly accumulated through the years may melt away, but the investment you have made in yourself, learning more, and enriching your personality, can never be taken from you. It lives on and on, paying dividends throughout the years.

In a large industrial plant one of the machines broke down and failed to operate. All work had to be stopped. The entire staff was laid off. An expert was called to repair the machine. The expert came, and with a little hammer, tapped here and tapped there. Finally, he announced that the machine was ready to operate. It did.

Later a bill arrived from the expert. It stated: "For Services Rendered—$200." A clerk in the accounting department sent back the bill, and asked for "an itemized statement of services rendered."

Back came the bill: "Itemized Statement for Services Rendered:

  For tapping power machine $ 1.00
  For knowing where to tap $199.00

7. Do You Have a Confidential Relationship with Someone Else?

Every person—no matter how young, how old, how rich, how poor, or how successful—needs *someone* to confide in, to talk to freely and without fear of being doublecrossed.

Loneliness is a cancer. A sorrow shared is always halved; a joy shared is always doubled.

A lady was alone in her home knitting peacefully when a telegram arrived telling her a distant cousin had passed away and left her a million dollars. Half the thrill of getting news like that, of course, comes from telling others about it. The little lady dropped her knitting, ran to the telephone, and cried excitedly, "Hello, operator! Get me anybody!"

A confidante may be a teacher, a priest, a rabbi, a mother, a father, a husband, a wife, a friend, or a psychiatrist. Some people need a listener so badly that they even get married to get one. Then, of course, often comes the greatest irony of all: the very person they married to be able to talk to freely and honestly is the person they start to lie to and to deceive. Could anything be more ironical?

A poor man passing a rich man saw him digging in his back yard.

"Why are you making a hole there?" the poor man asked.

"Because the Germans are coming, and I intend to bury my valuables, my candlesticks, silverware, before they get here."

A day later the rich man saw his poor neighbor digging in his own yard.

"Hey there, you haven't anything valuable. What are you digging a hole for?"

He looked up with indignation.

"Nothing valuable," he snorted. "I want you to understand that my wife is just as valuable to me as your fancy candlesticks and silverware."

8. *Do You Have a Sense of the Ridiculous?*

This is more than just a sense of humor. It implies the ability to be able to laugh at oneself. Can you look in the mirror for example and say to yourself, "My, what a little show-off I am. But I'm cute!"

Beware of feeling too important. Remember there is always someone who feels more important than you do. In a hospital for the mentally ill, a patient sat in the wards in a very grandiose pose. A psychiatrist passing by said to him, "Who do you think you are?"

"I, sir," answered the patient, "am Napoleon."

"Who told you that you were Napoleon?"

"God told me."

But a voice came from the next bed, "I DID NOT!"

Did you know that the more you laugh, the longer you laugh, and the easier it is to make you laugh, then the healthier is your personality? While you laugh you can't get ulcers. (Some of you are reading this too late!)

There was a man who at the age of 94 was the picture of health. Everyone marveled at his strength. They marveled all the more because it was well known that he had been married for over seventy years to a woman who had the temper of a shrew.

"How did you stay so healthy, married to such a woman?" an admirer asked him one day.

"Well," he drawled with a smile, "when my wife and I were married, we agreed that whenever we would quarrel, I would go out for a walk. Since the day I was married, I've been leading an *outdoor life!*"

The human body can never be angry and laugh at the same time. It is simply physically impossible.

Here is a little secret about human behavior that you can begin to use with good effects immediately. If your sweetheart, husband, or wife, is angry with you, and you are not (one of you must be not), and you wish to snap him out of his anger, it is very simple. Do one thing: make him laugh! If necessary, wiggle your ears at him, and you will be amazed at the results. (Of course, use good taste!)

9. *Are You Engaged in Satisfying Work?*

Satisfying work is a very strong and positive influence for mental hygiene. Satisfying work fulfills our innermost needs and gives us a strong prop with which to weather life's many frustrations. It supplies an outlet for our ego needs, and our creative interests.

No one ever broke down from "overstudy" or "overwork"—only from overworry!

Fortunate, indeed, is the person who discovers early what his niche in life should be, and who fights discouragement and thwarting in the attainment of his goal—and who eventually finds himself actively engaged for money in work that he would gladly do for nothing.

10. *Do You Attack Your Problems Promptly and Intelligently?*

"Don't make tragedies of trifles
Don't shoot butterflies with rifles."

I am always amused when I listen to some people advise their friends who are worried.

"Are you worried, Tom?"
"Oh yes."
"I'll tell you what to do."
"What?"
"DON'T WORRY!"

As if we could turn worry on and off like a faucet.

Or did you ever hear this beautiful gambit of advice to the troubled? "Are you troubled? I'll tell you what to do. Go to Florida for two months. Forget it."

I don't know whether you have ever realized it, but if you have a trouble inside you and you decide to go to Florida for two months, the trouble gets right on the train with you, goes straight to Florida—at no extra fare!

We are not *in* trouble; trouble is in us! "He who fights and runs away, will live to run again another day."

There is only one thing to do when you are worried, and this is it: DO SOMETHING ACTIVE ABOUT THE CAUSE OF YOUR WORRY. If you are worried about your physical health, then go to a doctor. Find out if your worries are justified. If you have an emotional problem, then seek out a psychiatrist.

"A psychiatrist!" say some, "a crazy doctor? Oh, no!"

When people begin to seek treatment for emotional problems as readily and as quickly as they do for physical problems, then we will have gone a long way to better prevention of personality breakdown.

Don't feel like the man who said, "Anyone who goes to a psychiatrist should have his head examined."

In solving your problems, get every assistance you can. Only when you have adequate knowledge are you in a position to make an intelligent decision. Remember too that it is often better to make a poor decision than to remain in a state of constant vacillation and indecision. This can rob you of all your energies.

Here is a personal illustration:

Recently, I remodeled a house. The contractor said to me, "Dr. Banks, what do you want—a square door or a round door?"

"Let me think about it a few days," I said.

I found that whenever I had to give a talk or was engaged in a conversation, I began to think, What should I do? Should I make it square or should I make it round? My powers of concentration were being affected, and were leaking out through the worry.

I immediately phoned the contractor and said, "For Heaven's sake, make it square!"

"Are you sure you don't want it round?" he asked.

"Don't even talk to me about it." I hung up and felt better at once.

What would have happened had I gone to a movie in an attempt to forget my problem?

If the hero should say to the heroine, "Come now, kiss me—give me a square deal"—what do you think I would have thought about first? You're right!—Should I make it square, or should I make it round?

Ah, but what does one do when one can't do something active about the cause of worry? Then, of course, you must develop what are called "balancing factors." What is a "balancing factor?" A story will make it clear.

Bing Crosby's little boy was feeling very sad. His pet turtle was dying, and he was almost inconsolable.

Bing tried to cheer him up, and said, "Look, son, if the turtle dies, do you know what we'll do? We'll put him in a little box, get all the kids together, put on fancy uniforms, get a bugle, march down the street in a parade, and bury him in the back yard."

The boy listened carefully, hesitated and then said, "Let's kill him!"

The Quest for Happiness

Life itself is very much like climbing a slippery glass hill. We climb, and we slip; we climb a little more, and slip again. *We all slip!* Everyone has sorrow, disappointment, tragedy, frustration! But the measure of a man—the measure of you—is not whether you slip, but what you do when you slip.

Do you pick yourself up and go a little higher on the hill, or do you lie there and whine, or go backward into illness, nervous breakdown?

Never forget that happiness is like a butterfly. The more you chase it and chase it *directly*—then the more it will elude you. But if you sit down quietly and turn your attention to other things—then it comes and softly sits on your shoulder!

DR. MURRAY BANKS
Eight East 63 Street   New York 21, New York

℞ *Slow Down*

Certainly, you are busy. Work is piling up and you fume and fuss and pitch in and work, but it piles even higher. What the heck! SLOW DOWN. You could live to be as old as Methuselah and still find work piling up on you.

One man, harried, hurried, and explosive over his work, was advised to work six hours per day instead of eight and also spend one day a week in the cemetery.

"But what shall I do in the cemetery?"

"Just loaf," was the reply, "Get acquainted with some of the men who are there permanently. They didn't finish their work either. Nobody does, you know."

So — SLOW-DOWN — today — and enjoy life — before YOU go down — permanently.

A "PILL IN PRINT" – TURN OVER

"PILLS" IN PRINT BY DR. MURRAY BANKS

1. **"HOW TO LIVE WITH YOURSELF"** $1
   One of the most provocative and witty prescriptions ever written. Packed with thoughts to keep you smiling while suggesting a way of life that you wish you had thought of long ago.

2. **"WHAT TO DO UNTIL THE PSYCHIATRIST COMES"** $1
   A dramatic and humorous presentation on little known and exciting things about life. Sparkling humor and rollicking stories walk hand in hand with a fascinating look into the human mind.

3. **"JUST IN CASE YOU THINK YOU'RE NORMAL"** $1
   The title speaks for itself. You will laugh and learn while learning to do both.

4. **"HOW TO OVERCOME AN INFERIORITY COMPLEX"** $1
   Order some for your friends. It will be a treat as well as a treatment!

5. **"STOP THE WORLD, I WANT TO GET OFF!" OR "HOW TO RUB SHOULDERS WITH HAPPINESS"** $1
   Contains a formula of six wonder tablets, compounded with a heavy sugar coating that will make the swallowing most pleasant, and assure you of some fascinating shoulder-rubbing.

12" LP RECORDS BY DR. MURRAY BANKS

1. **"HOW TO LIVE WITH YOURSELF" OR "WHAT TO DO UNTIL THE PSYCHIATRIST COMES"** $5.98
   This is one of the most popular talks ever given in America. Given over 5,000 times, it has stirred audiences to cheers.
   The drama of life is unfolded to you with charm and wit, helping you learn the secret of the most difficult art in the world... how to live with yourself!

2. **"JUST IN CASE YOU THINK YOU'RE NORMAL!"** $5.98
   A fascinating medley of humor, psychology, flavorsome stories and dramatic case histories unfold the everyday problems of life. A talk guaranteed to brighten dull moments and to ease your problems.

3. **"THE DRAMA OF SEX"** $5.98
   A complete capsule course in sex education, delivered frankly, accurately, and in the humorous style of Dr. Banks.

4. **"DR. MURRAY BANKS TELLS JEWISH STORIES MIT PSYCHOLOGY"** $5.98
   Contains a collection of hilarious stories given in Yiddish and English. For those who understand the language, there is an hour of guaranteed bellylaughs! Knowledge of Yiddish required.

5. **"DR. MURRAY BANKS TELLS MORE JEWISH STORIES MIT PSYCHOLOGY"** $5.98
   A great collection of the best Jewish humor, all in English, to tickle the risibilities of the Cohens and the Murphys... all this, and psychology too!

6. **"A LESSON IN LOVE"** $5.98
   The psychology of love and marriage, difference between love and infatuation, how to get the one you want to fall in love with you, and other exciting secrets of a subject that fascinates everyone.

MOST TIMELY AND VALUABLE TALK

7. **"HOW TO QUIT SMOKING IN SIX DAYS... OR DROP DEAD IN SEVEN!"** $5.98
   A bright and humorous presentation of a deadly serious problem. Dr. Banks explains why people smoke, how it affects mind and body, how a person becomes addicted, and finally presents the only sure way to "get the monkey off your back." A valuable talk for all adults, and a MUST for teenagers.
   Especially important for those who haven't yet started to smoke!

MURMIL ASSOCIATES, INC., 8 East 63rd Street, New York, N. Y. 10021

Use this handy order form to get your copies of Dr. Murray Banks publications and/or special LP 33⅓ phonograph records.

Mail with your remittance to:

Murmil Associates, Inc.
Eight East 63rd Street
New York, New York 10021

Gentlemen:

Please send the following "pills" in print and/or phonograph records by Dr. Murray Banks:

PILLS IN PRINT

- [ ] 1. How to Live With Yourself.............................$1
- [ ] 2. What to Do Until the Psychiatrist Comes.................$1
- [ ] 3. Just In Case You Think You're Normal...................$1
- [ ] 4. How to Overcome An Inferiority Complex................$1
- [ ] 5. Stop the World, I Want to Get Off! or How to Rub Shoulders With Happiness.................................$1

LP 33⅓ RECORDS

- [ ] 1. How to Live With Yourself — or — What to Do Until the Psychiatrist Comes $5.98
- [ ] 2. Just in Case You Think You're Normal...............$5.98
- [ ] 3. The Drama of Sex................................$5.98
- [ ] 4. Dr. Murray Banks tells Jewish Stories Mit Psychology (Knowledge of Yiddish Required)....................$5.98
- [ ] 5. Dr. Murray Banks tells more Jewish Stories Mit Psychology $5.98
- [ ] 6. A Lesson in Love................................$5.98
- [ ] 7. How to Quit Smoking in Six Days... or Drop Dead in Seven $5.98

I am enclosing $..................

Name..

Address...

City.................................... State......................Zip..................

Please cut on this line.